Welcome to
Wee Cumbrae

A pictorial stroll around Wee Cumbrae.
By Ardrossan based authors John and Noreen Steele.

John Steele

Noreen Steele

Reviews by
Jill McColl
The Vennel Local and Family History Centre
North Ayrshire Council
and
Donald L Reid. Author and local historian. Beith.

First published in the United Kingdom, 2009
By John and Noreen Steele

Enquiries regarding book sales to:
John and Noreen Steele
104 Eglinton Road
Ardrossan
North Ayrshire
Scotland
KA22 8NN

E: j.steele2@talktalk.net

ISBN: 978-0-9532637-0-7

Designed and printed in Great Britain by
Cleland Crosbie Limited Printers, Beith, Ayrshire, Scotland
Tel: 01505-504848

Acknowledgments

The authors are grateful to the following individuals for their helpful assistance in making this book possible. Graham Wilson, photographer, Saltcoats; for accompanying us on our sojourn and taking such brilliant photographs. Mrs Jean Horn; for her generous hospitality to us on our frequent visits to Millport. Jean shared her memories as a lighthouse keeper's wife and allowed the use of her precious collection of photographs. Brothers Jack and Ronnie Horn; for recalling their happy lives as young boys on Wee Cumbrae and providing valuable photographs. Kenny McNeill, Navigation Aids Engineer, Clydeport Operations, Greenock; for his unreserved assistance in our research, allowing us to photograph the gramophone record and poster regarding the talking beacon. Donald L Reid author and local historian Beith; for his invaluable advice and support, always freely given.

Mark Strachan North Ayrshire Museum Saltcoats; for locating historical items of interest for this book. Jim McCauley Area Librarian Saltcoats Library; always our first port of call when a helping hand is required.

Caretakers of Wee Cumbrae Island, Al and Bonnie Davidson; for their kind hospitality and information about the island. Jim Oliver ex-lighthouse keeper; who detailed the lighthouse keeper duties for us. The staff at the Vennel Local and Family History Centre Irvine; for their helpful assistance in our research. Charles and Sheila Murray, Rothesay, Isle of Bute; for the use of the circa 1654 map of the Cumbrae's. Doctor Christine Lodge and staff, Ayrshire Archives Centre, Ayr; for finding and providing historical information. Author Joan Biggar Ardrossan; for her encouragement and guidance in our project.

We also express gratitude to Caledonian MacBrayne (CalMac) Gourock. Cathedral of the Isles Millport. The Bulletin. The Garrison Millport. Greenock Telegraph. Largs and Millport Weekly News. Scottish Maritime Museum Irvine. McLean Museum and Art Gallery Greenock. Museum of Scottish Lighthouses Fraserburgh. RSPB Lochwinnoch. University of Glasgow. Watt Library Greenock. Castle House Museum Dunoon. Cleland Crosbie Limited, Printers, Beith.

Index of Photographs

Grandparents John and Noreen Steele with grandchildren. At back Kirsten and Robbie. Left to right Blair, Ramsay, Sally, Harrison, Campbell and Finlay.

Other books published by John Steele and Noreen Steele:
The Tragedy of HMS Dasher.
They Were Never Told.
The Secrets of HMS Dasher.
Burning Ships.
Whispers of Horse Island.

Welcome to
Wee Cumbrae

Millport on the island of Great Cumbrae, situated in the Firth of Clyde, is an extremely popular holiday destination. Nestled nearby is the tiny island of Wee Cumbrae. Although this small island is all but unnoticed it has a fascinating history.

Over the years the names of both islands have frequently changed. The bigger of the two islands was originally named Kumbra Moir becoming Greater Cumray, through the years this became Great Cumbrae, and it is now referred to as Big Cumbrae.

The small island was originally named Kumbra Beg becoming Little Cumray then Lesser Cumbrae, now commonly known as Wee Cumbrae.

This island extends to 684 acres, is 1.8 miles long and at its widest point is only 0.9 miles.

Most of the island is surrounded by sheer coastal cliffs. Walking across the island from coast to coast involves a very steep climb. The ground covering is lush because of the warmth of the Gulf Stream. There are also a few lochans.

There is a very long history of human occupation which is confirmed by Prehistoric, Bronze and Iron Age archaeological remains. Wee Cumbrae has more than 100 place names of Scots, Shetland, Gaelic, Danish, and Norse origins emphasising its diverse cultural history.

The word Cumbrae is derived from the Gaelic meaning safety or refuge and it was for this reason that the Missionary Saint Beya is reputed to have landed on the island in the 7th century. Saint Beya was an Irish princess who was betrothed, against her will, to the King of Norway's son. She fled the court as she had always desired to devote her life to Christ. Saint Beya was an early Christian missionary, known as The Maiden, who was a devout follower of Saint Columba of Iona. During the seventh century Saint Beya arrived at the small island with the intention of locating the most peaceful and serene part of the island for the building of a small chapel and retreat. It was built beside a rocky natural amphitheatre amidst an abundance of bracken. The building measured only 42 feet in length and 20 feet wide. Inside it was equally divided; the front half was the chapel, the rear half being where Saint Beya lived and prayed. Saint Beya was held in such high esteem that it is recorded; *an army of men came to hear her preach*.

The legend of Saint Beya carried on throughout the centuries. In bygone times local legend suggests that Wee Cumbrae Island became a place of pilgrimage equal to Iona.

There are several caves on the island. One large cave, with a hidden entrance, is 100 feet in length. Within the cave are high, dry ledges suitable to sleep on. Here the monks of Saint Beya took refuge in times of danger.

When Saint Beya passed away, in accordance with her wishes, she was buried on the island close to her beloved chapel. She was held in such high esteem a poem of many verses was written. Two of the verses read;

> In perfect calm and meditative mood
> She daily sought by prayer and fastings oft
> The venerable Beya, whose remains
> In that same isle were decently interred.
> Forthwith a chapel in her honour rose
> And pious pilgrims to it came in troops.

> As if the sight of their old teacher's grave
> Would quicken their devotions, and create
> A sense of joyous comfort in their prayers.
> So with the circling years the custom grew
> To have some play or game on our saint's day.

Throughout the years Saint Beya's chapel gradually became a ruin but still the pilgrims came to pay their respects to the maiden saint. On arrival at the island the pilgrims landed on a small sandy beach known as C*ravies Hole* or *Creek of the Devout Folk* and were directed to the chapel as follows; *Let the traveller turn past the farm house, keeping to the right. Proceed north to the old ruined barn. Walk in a northerly direction for three hundred yards then turn sharply to the left. Turn slightly to the right then walk westwards for eighty yards. Having walked less than one mile from the sea-shore, partly uphill, the traveller will find themselves at the Chapel of Saint Beya.*

During the 12th century work commenced to build a castle on a small tidal islet. The walls which were 6.5 feet thick had narrow openings for the firing of arrows. Entrance was gained by means of a drawbridge. The interior consisted of a basement and three floors.

In the spring of 1375 King Robert 11 took up residence in Cumbrae Castle to enjoy a season of fishing and hunting. During his stay many Royal Charters were signed then sealed with the royal seal and stamped **Cumbrae Castle**. The King returned for another season in 1384 to enjoy his sporting interests and his temporary retirement from public life. Once more he signed Royal Charters at Cumbrae Castle. Later King Robert 111 also enjoyed many relaxing visits to Little Cumbrae.

During the 1450s the castle custodian was Robert Hunter of Hunterston, a wealthy land owner who resided on the mainland directly across from Wee Cumbrae Island. In 1515 Hugh Montgomerie 1st Earl of Eglinton was appointed by the government Privy Council who made him custodian of Little Cumbrae Island and Castle.

After accepting custodianship of Little Cumbrae Island the wealthy Earl of Eglinton purchased it from the Crown. The earl's main residence was the prestigious Eglinton Castle in North Ayrshire. He also owned Ardrossan Castle.

In 1568 Hugh Montgomerie 3rd Earl of Eglinton wrote a letter of contract addressed to a Glassin Right (a glazier) in Glasgow. The letter was accepting the glazier's quotation to maintain the windows at the Earl's three castles. In return every year the glazier would receive from the earl two bags of oats and two stone of cheese. During the time of his employment he would receive his meals and also have the use of a horse and carriage to transport the glass from Glasgow.

In the early1650s Alexander Montgomerie 6th Earl of Eglinton was alerted that Cromwell's army was heading north to pillage Ardrossan Castle. The Earl hastily departed from Ardrossan and sought refuge at his castle on Little Cumbrae. Three years later Cromwell's army returned to the west of Scotland, sailed across the Firth of Clyde to Little Cumbrae and ransacked the castle. Prior to departing from the island the English army set the castle alight. With a population of only eight on the island there was no resistance to the invading English army.

In 1813 Archibald William Montgomerie 13th Earl of Eglinton turned his attention to the many prehistoric, Bronze and Iron Age archaeological remains. He ordered that some of the burial places on the island should be excavated. When the largest burial cairn was opened his men found a heavy sword of great length. The handle had an iron guard to protect the hand and wrist. The workmen also uncovered a full set of armour, including the breast plate and a helmet with a visor. Another sword was found to be very badly corroded and when an attempt was made to lift it by the handle it fell into small pieces.

During the 1850s George Montgomerie 15th Earl of Eglinton ordered his gamekeeper to introduce rabbits to the island. Within a few years the earl's plan reached fruition when the gamekeeper reported that the island was over-run by rabbits. This allowed the Earl of Eglinton to rent out the island to parties of shooters thereby accruing finance to help towards the running of his estate. With over 5,000 rabbits a year being bred on the island rabbit-shooting became a popular sport. During this period the population of the island was twenty five.

Over the years the population comprised of crofters who also fished for herring, a local shepherd, farm workers, lighthouse keepers and their families. The population varied with the size of the lighthouse keeper's families.

The lighthouse keepers and their families enjoyed the peace and tranquillity offered by the island. They were housed beside the lighthouse and had a huge walled garden. The landing jetty, situated beneath the lighthouse was never easy to access as it had no shelter from the wild sea and winds. The keepers' families were frequently cut off from Great Cumbrae due to adverse weather. The keeper's wives had to keep their larders always well stocked as the delivery of fresh supplies depended on the weather.

The children attended school in Millport and were boarded there Monday to Friday. They returned home each weekend, weather permitting.

Unfortunately tragedy struck on 17th March 1893 when a keeper was returning to the island with four of his children and the boat capsized. Two of the children drowned and the other two died shortly afterwards.

William Alexander Montgomerie, 17th Earl of Eglinton sold the island to Mr Evelyn Parker in 1931 for the sum of £5,000. During their ownership the Parker family carried out many improvements, alterations and substantial extensions to the stone farmhouse. No expense was spared when Mr Evelyn Parker commissioned Gertrude Jekyll to design and create a beautiful garden. Gertrude Jekyll had already designed and laid out more than 400 gardens in Britain, Europe and America. During the garden design and development boat loads of the best top-soil were shipped to the island.

On completion of the horticultural work Mr Parker's prestigious mansion was now set amidst one of the best gardens in Scotland.

The owner utilised the island as a working farm by shipping in sheep and cattle. They were allowed to roam freely and graze on the lush growth before being returned to the mainland to be sold at the market.

Life on the island was greatly enhanced when on 8th May 1957 Wee Cumbrae received an electric supply via a sea-bed cable from Great Cumbrae.

It became increasingly popular for the residents on the nearby island of Great Cumbrae to sail over to Wee Cumbrae to enjoy a day trip. During their visit to the island the day trippers treated themselves to tea and home baking, which was served by a keeper's wife Sadie Hill from her kitchen window.

When Mr Evelyn Parker passed away he was buried on the island. His son sold Wee Cumbrae in 1960 to Mr Peter Kaye, for the sum of £24,000.

In the early 1960s the last three lighthouse keepers, stationed with their families, were Roy Horn, Archie Sinclair and Alec Clark. Their large walled garden was well tended and kept the families provided with fresh fruit and vegetables. When the navigation light was automated in 1974 the lighthouse keepers with their families left the island for the last time to be re-housed in Millport.

In 2002 Mr Steven Worrallo of Holt Enterprises, Worcestershire, purchased the island and engaged two caretakers, Al and Bonnie Davidson.

To this day the island remains in private ownership.

In July 2009 Wee Cumbrae was sold reputedly for £2million. The new owners are Glasgow businessman Sam Podder and his wife Sunita.

Little Cumbrae Castle is situated on the east coast of the island. It stands prominently on Castle Island, which is tidal allowing easy access at low tide.

Due to the ever increasing volume of shipping negotiating the entrance to the River Clyde, it was deemed necessary to erect a navigation light on Little Cumbrae.

The Cumry Lighthouse Act was passed in parliament on the 15th April 1756. It sanctioned the construction of a lighthouse on Little Cumbrae and resulted in the very first lighthouse being built in the Clyde. The Act also stated; *The Trustees of Little Cumry Lighthouse shall be paid one penny sterling per ton for every British ship and two pence per ton for every foreign vessel that passes the light.*

In 1756 construction commenced, at the highest point 409 feet above sea level, of a 30 foot high coal fired tower. It took a year to build the tower, a keeper's cottage and also a rough track from the jetty up the hillside to the tower. The appointed keepers were Peter Montgomerie and Thomas Fairie. The fire at the top of the tower was lit for the first time on the 8th December 1757.

A constant supply of coal was required to fuel the tower fire. The coal was unloaded at the jetty near the castle. Donkeys were used to pull the carts carrying the coal up the steep hill to the light tower.

A round iron basket was fixed at the top of the round tower. Coal had to be manually carried up the internal circular stairway and thrown into the basket. Every evening the coal was lit and remained so until dawn. The light from the flames of the fire was the navigation aid. On clear nights the fire burned brightly, shining across the shipping lanes around the island.

Unfortunately, due to the high position of the lighthouse low cloud and mist regularly obscured the flames. To compound matters when it was raining it proved very difficult to keep the fire alight.

The transportation of tons of coal to the port at Irvine then shipping it across the Firth of Clyde was becoming too costly. Throughout the years as the light keepers struggled to maintain the hill top beacon the trustees tried to find a solution to improving the aid to navigation in the area. Eventually it was decided to construct a new oil fired lighthouse on the cliff top on the west coast.

The new lighthouse, along with ancillary buildings, were constructed on the large area of flat ground on the high cliff top. Substantial cottages were built to house the lighthouse keepers and their families. There were always three keepers stationed there, a principle keeper with two assistants. The principle keeper's house was attached to the lighthouse for easy access.

The whole lighthouse complex was surrounded by a large wall which gave protection to the keepers sizable gardens.

The lighthouse was built by a local contractor named Anderson. The reflecting light was manufactured at Smith's workshop in Glasgow. It had 32 whale oil lamps with glass reflectors.

The construction of this second lighthouse went according to schedule. After 36 years of being in operation the light tower's coal fire was lit for the last time on the 30th September 1793. The new lighthouse came into operation the following evening, 1st October 1793 and proved to be very successful as the light could be seen by mariners from a distance of 16 miles.

33 years later in 1826 the Stevensons (of whom RL Stevenson was a descendent) were contracted to replace the light with 15 argand lights and silver reflectors after which the light could be picked up from 30 miles distant.

In 1858 a diaphone fog horn operated by compressed air was fitted in addition to the light.

In the year 1900 the whale oil fuelled lamps were replaced by a wet cell battery powered electric light. This was only used for eight years before being replaced by a more efficient acetylene gas light.

The walled lighthouse complex has over 90 steps leading 100 feet down the cliff face to two landing stages. Although not well sheltered the small one was essential for the use of the keeper's boat. This was their only means of reaching Great Cumbrae to bring in supplies and ferry the children to school. The larger landing stage was for the supply vessel. High on the hill, directly above still stands the coal fired beacon tower. It was in use for 36 years until replaced by the lighthouse.

The landing stage on the left for the keepers small boat is completely covered by the wild sea. On the right of the boathouse is the large jetty for the supply vessel. The keepers' wives were always prepared for times when stores could not be brought out to them.
(Bute is seen in the background)

On the 17th March 1893 lighthouse keeper James Wallace set off on the short voyage to Millport in a lugsail (a rowing boat with a small sail). Four of his five children were attending school there. The parents were anxious to have their children home as they had been stranded in Millport for 3 weeks because of stormy weather.

On the return journey they encountered a terrible squall. In the lighthouse the children's mother and assistant lighthouse keeper Angus Kerr anxiously watched the heavily laden small craft struggling in the unsheltered water. The children firmly gripped their seats as a gust of wind caught the sail. Suddenly the small boat capsized throwing everyone into the cold water. With wild waves washing over them James Wallace clung on to 9 year old Jessie, his other daughter 15 year old Netta managed to stay afloat.

Sadly 13 year old Alex and 11 year old John disappeared under the waves dragged down by the weight of their heavy school bags which were slung over their shoulders. Meantime in the lighthouse the children's mother and Angus Kerr witnessed the tragedy and rushed down to the jetty to reach the small boat then rowed as quickly as possible to help. On reaching the scene they pulled the exhausted girls and their dad out of the water.

With three safely onboard they all looked frantically for signs of the two missing boys but it was hopeless.

They then headed as fast as possible to Millport. Before reaching the pier tragically little Jessie succumbed to the cold.

When they landed the local GP Doctor McGown was waiting for them and tried to save Netta but it was in vain, the fourth child passed away. Completely exhausted and distraught the father was carried into the Royal George Hotel at the pier head.

It was a dreadful day for the islands of Little Cumbrae and Great Cumbrae when the children were buried in Cumbrae Cemetery. Millport. A memorial stone was later erected with the engraved words:

The teachers and scholars of Cumbrae Primary School.
In loving memory of Netta, Alexander, John and Jessie Wallace
who were accidently drowned on the 17th March 1893.
There is a happy land far far away.

Over the years many shipping vessels have come to grief on the rocky shores of Little Cumbrae. Brigs, barques, schooners, lugsails, puffers, steamships, passenger ships, merchant ships, dredgers, rowing boats and many other leisure craft have all fallen foul of the island. Launched in the Clyde in 1882 at McMillan's shipyard Dumbarton, the cargo sailing ship *Lady Isabella* was nearing the end of a long three month journey from the South Pacific. On entering the Firth of Clyde on the 27th August, 1902, the 2000 ton iron barque was experiencing great difficulty due to an ever worsening storm. When the vessel was approaching Little Cumbrae the wind rose ferociously and ripped clean through the sails rendering them completely useless. Now at the mercy of the violent squall the huge waves carried the cargo ship ever closer to the rocky south west coast of the island. Captain McKinley and his crew fought valiantly in an attempt to avoid the treacherous rocks but it was all to no avail. The doomed ship crashed hard aground onto the jagged rocks, within sight of the lighthouse. A brave crewman volunteered to swim the short distance to the island with a rescue line. He reached the rocky shore and secured the line then managed to haul all his shipmates ashore. When the ship was later examined by divers it was deemed to be a total wreck.

The *Montclare*, a majestic Clyde built passenger liner was launched on the 18th December 1921 at John Brown's Shipyard. For ten years the ship had an unblemished career until Saturday 21st March 1931. On that fateful day the *Montclare* had nearly completed her voyage from Canada to Glasgow. Since entering the Firth of Clyde speed had been reduced to Dead Slow due to dense fog. At 2pm all was well until suddenly straight ahead Wee Cumbrae loomed out of the fog. The passengers and crew heard grating sounds as the ship's bottom scraped along the rocks then there was a horrendous crunching noise which brought the ship to a stop. The passenger ship was firmly aground on the west side of the island.

Onboard the stranded vessel more than 300 passengers were being assured by the officers that there was no cause for alarm and that the ship would soon be afloat. At the arrival of the rescue tugs the passengers lined the decks to watch them working in unison trying to refloat their ship.

Unfortunately the tide was receding and the stranded ship was settling down more on the rocky shore. As the tide went out the passenger ship listed heavily at a dangerous angle and in the interest of safety the captain gave the order:

"Abandon Ship"

The scene was now dramatic as the lifeboats were lowered and began ferrying the passengers to safety on the island. Once ashore the tugs were waiting to transport the passengers to Largs Pier. After all the passengers were transferred the tugs returned to the stricken ship. When the tide was at its highest the *Montclare* was towed successfully off the rocks by four tugs.

After being refloated the ship's hull was examined and it was found that the only damage sustained was to the starboard propeller.

The cargo vessel *SS Rockpool* had achieved an illustrious career since being built in 1927. She had even come under attack by a German U-boat in October 1939. Rather than flee the scene Captain Harland ordered his gunner to return fire. For over an hour battle raged with the U-boat submerging and surfacing three times. Finally the U-boat was left badly damaged and unable to submerge. Captain Harland left it to be finished off by a Royal Navy destroyer the following day.

Two years later the *SS Rockpool* had once more run the gauntlet across the Atlantic before entering safely into home waters. As the ship was heading at speed for Greenock she inexplicably smashed into the island of Wee Cumbrae and was declared a complete wreck.

The ship that had survived enemy mines and aircraft fire plus winning a battle against U-boat came to a tragic end on this little island.

By now the Ministry of War being desperate for ships had the wrecked hull towed to a Clyde shipyard and completely rebuilt. Launched as *HMS Empire Trent* the warship was involved in active war service then later used as a submarine depot ship at Rothesay, a few miles from where she had been wrecked.

August 1964. These two boats belonged to the island's owner Mr Peter Kaye. The barge, partly beached, was used to transport cattle and sheep to and from the island. The other vessel is the *Jeannie Speirs* an ex RNLI lifeboat which had been based at Portpatrick from 1937-1961. During 24 years active service it was launched 66 times saving 18 lives.

This beach is where the pilgrims of Saint Beya are reputed to have landed.

The landing stage at the foot of the cliff beneath the lighthouse complex. Everything needed for life on the island was unloaded here. When spare parts and heavy goods were landed the concrete jetty was used by the supply vessel *Torch*. When the children were being ferried to and from school in the small launch they made use of the smaller jetty with steps.

The supply vessel *Torch* alongside the jetty delivering goods from the mainland. Supplies such as fan belts, filters, diesel, lubricating oil and cleaning material for the generators are being hoisted up the cliff face and over the complex wall. The three lighthouse keepers are watching the unloading operation with interest and enjoying a chat with the crew of the supply ship.

The *Torch* was a multi-purpose ship involved in the maintenance of buoys, shore lights, oil spillage support, towage, hydrographic surveys, salvage and diving support. It was also used to move the keeper's household belongings when he was assigned to another lighthouse.

On the 31st January 1931 the Clyde Lighthouses Trustees announced the introduction of a Talking Beacon at Little Cumbrae Lighthouse The Notice to Mariners poster giving instructions regarding the talking beacon. (This notice is still on display at Clydeport Greenock.)

This new innovation comprised of a gramophone record being played over the radio when the fog horn was in operation. Any vessel having the simplest ship-to-shore radio was able to pick up the message transmitted from Cumbrae Lighthouse. The ship's radio operator would then immediately know the distance his ship was from the lighthouse. The Talking Beacon record was recorded by EMI Studios Ltd. London. When played a commanding voice is heard speaking the following:

Cumbrae

one two three four five six seven eight nine

After one ring of a bell the voice states:

One mile!

This is then repeated another four times counting up to five miles.

After a visit keeper Archie Sinclair's brother-in-law is returning to Millport. Taking advantage of the good weather Jean Horn takes her son Ronnie and Dorothy Clark along for the trip. Dorothy's dad is in charge of the boat.

January 1965. The lighthouse keeper's small power boat being winched out of the water into the boat house The sea must have been relatively calm as Jean Horn had joined her husband on a shopping trip to Millport. The boat had a small canvas hood which could be pulled into position when it was raining. A cabin was later fitted to afford proper shelter.
The white building in the background was the gas store.

Two lighthouse keepers returning from a shopping trip to Millport. Archie Sinclair is carrying the milk and Alec Clark is carrying groceries on his shoulder. On arrival in Millport the keepers would hand in a shopping list to the shops. The shopkeeper would pack up the shopping and deliver it to the pier.

October 1965. Jack and Ronnie Horn with Dorothy Clark in their cart. The cart was also used to transport the shopping up the hill.

Lighthouse keeper Roy Horn made great use of his camera. He recorded life on the island during the 1960s giving a great insight into the lives of the keepers and their families. On or off duty the keepers were always busy. There was cleaning and maintenance to attend to. Everything had to be kept in perfect working order. Tending the large garden and grass cutting was an added chore during summer.

The Horn family Jack and Ronnie with their parents Roy and Jean spending a pleasant afternoon fishing off the rocks whilst their Dad is off duty.

January 1965. Mrs Jean Horn escorting visitors up the sheep track which leads up and over to the other side of the island.

August 1964. Outside Jean Horn's house. Edna Sinclair, Neil the occasional keeper (Stand-in for holidays), Jean holding Karen Sinclair and Mrs Sinclair. In front Andrew, Jack and Ronnie.

The families all got on really well together. They enjoyed picnics when other family members came to visit. From the left they are
Mrs Mary Sinclair, her son Kenny, his wife Edna, their daughter Karen and Jean Horn whose husband Roy is as usual behind the camera.

October 1965. Birthday boys Jack Horn and Ronnie Clark. The two boys have a joint birthday party. Both age 7 years. The best china is in use for this special occasion.

January 1965. Keeper Alec Clark's children Ronnie and Dorothy looking very innocent.

October 1965 "The Wee Cumbrae Cycling Club."
From left on the bikes. Dorothy Clark, Jack Horn, Ronnie Clark and Ronnie Horn. Two associate members Karen and Andrew Sinclair with no bikes yet.

August 1964. The keepers were always smartly dressed on or off duty. Here keeper Archie Sinclair is showing off a huge eel he has caught. In the background is the World's first flashing sea buoy which began service adjacent to Wee Cumbrae in 1880. After being decommissioned it was hoisted up and over the wall to be placed on the front lawn. The buoy's original colours consisted of three broad stripes. Red at the top, black at the bottom with white in between.
On arrival at the lighthouse as it was badly in need of a fresh coat of paint the lighthouse keepers painted it black. It was removed to Greenock promenade where it is on display with its original colours restored.

August 1964. Ronnie closely examines the large eel still hooked on the line. Jack stands back, taking precautions, in case the monster slithers up his leg.

September 1965. Jack Horn age 7 prepares for the hunt. Here he is looking very knowledgeable "breaking" his father's shotgun. Rabbits beware!
(The shotgun is not loaded)

Jack and Ronnie Horn enjoying a rough and tumble in the walled garden. The walls are lined with fruit bushes, which provided an abundant harvest for the keeper's wives jam making sessions. Each of the three wives had their own drying green with four clothes poles as seen here.

August 1964. Ronnie follows big brother Jack on a hill climbing venture. Notice how their mother Jean always managed to have them so well turned out, even to the creases in their little trousers.

There are two ways to reach Wee Cumbrae both from the busy town of Largs. The direct way is via a charter boat over to the island. We decided on the more leisurely way by taking the CalMac ferry over to Big Cumbrae. This would allow us time to stop by some of the places of interest before continuing on to Wee Cumbrae.

As we planned to do a circular tour on our day trip our return to Largs would be on the vintage boat *Silver Spray*.

We boarded *Loch Shira at* Largs for the short 10 minute sail across the busy shipping lane. The *Loch Shira* is capable of carrying 35 cars and 250 passengers and is one of Cal Mac's latest roll-on roll-off ferries.

Arriving at the island's slipway on Big Cumbrae. There is always a line of cars waiting to board for the return journey. We join the passengers who all scurry off the ferry with most heading towards the waiting bus.

The bus winds its way along the coast road for four miles into Millport the only town on the island. As the roads twists and turns the changing views across to the mainland are really impressive. The bus travels round the whole sweep of Millport bay to reach its destination at the pier head.

The picturesque main street of Millport as viewed from the harbour. Millport is ideal for a traditional family seaside holiday. There is a safe sandy beach for bathing and the favoured mode of transport is the bicycle. There always seems to be dozens of cyclists pedalling their way round the island.

The Crocodile Rock sits on the seafront at Millport and has been a source of fascination to children for many years. The rock was first painted during the early 1900s. The artistic paintwork is touched-up frequently, resulting in this fearsome creature becoming a permanent attraction on the beach.

The jougs (chain and manacle) now hang on the pillar at the entrance to Millport Old Cemetery. During the 15th century it was a means of punishment. The jougs were fixed to the rocks with the unfortunate prisoner attached. It was similar in use to the stocks. The offender was put on view to the public and therefore open to ridicule and humiliation.

This little house is known as the Wedge, because it is shaped like a wedge of cheese. Remarkably this house is recorded in the Guinness Book of World Records as having the narrowest frontage in the world. Built in 1875 the frontage width is only 47 inches.
On the ground floor there is a kitchen / lounge. The upper floor comprises of one bedroom and a bathroom.

SCOTTISH
EPISCOPAL CHURCH
DIOCESE OF ARGYLL AND THE ISLES

CATHEDRAL OF THE ISLES
AND
COLLEGE OF THE HOLY SPIRIT

SERVICES
SUNDAY 11 AM - SUNG EUCHARIST
OTHER SERVICES - SEE PORCH NOTICE BOARD

PROVOST -
PRIEST-IN-CHARGE -
WARDEN -

THE CATHEDRAL IS OPEN DAILY
ACCOMMODATION IS AVAILABLE
AT THE COLLEGE
ENQUIRIES - 01475 530353

The cathedral information board is situated on the left of the main pathway leading through the tranquil grounds to the cathedral.

The Cathedral of the Isles is the smallest cathedral in Europe. Founded by the Hon. George Frederick Boyle, 6th Earl of Glasgow. The architecturally outstanding building was completed in 1852. Four years later the building was consecrated as Cathedral of the Isles. It has seating for barely 100.

The interior of the cathedral is remarkably well maintained and looks loved and well cared for. This beautiful little cathedral attracts a constant stream of visitors.

IN AFFECTIONATE REMEMBRANCE
OF GEORGE HODGE AND HIS SON
WILLIAM FERGUSON, LOST OFF
LESSER CUMBRAE, SEPT. 21ST 1878.
I WILL BRING MINE OWN AGAIN FROM THE DEPTHS OF THE SEA

The memorial plaque mounted inside the cathedral commemorates the loss of a father and his son off Wee Cumbrae. The tragedy occurred when two adults, four boys and a servant girl were on board a small sailing boat near to Wee Cumbrae. Unfortunately the weather changed and the sea became rough causing the small boat to capsize and sink.

Lighthouse keeper Archibald McNielage witnessed the incident and without hesitation he bravely rowed out to help and managed to pull on board Mrs Hodge, three boys and the servant girl. Mr Hodge and his son sadly drowned.

Garrison House was built by Commander James Crawford. It later became the family home of Lord Glasgow the then owner of the island. The building was devastated by fire in 2001 and lay derelict for five years until a major restoration programme commenced in 2006. Two years later the building was officially opened and now houses the library, museum, café, NHS health centre, tourist information and council office. This excellent building restored to its former glory is now the heart of the community.

One of the original reflectors from the lighthouse is on display in Garrison House Millport. Every morning one of the duties of the lighthouse keeper was to dust the reflectors with a feather before gently cleaning them with a soft cloth.

Millport Bay looking to the mainland of North Ayrshire. Seals are regular visitors to the bay. The blue fishing boat *Dawn Rise* is moored at the jetty waiting for us to board and set sail to Wee Cumbrae.

The approach to Wee Cumbrae is quite spectacular. The landing jetty, boat house, slipway and an adjacent storage building are seen on the right hand side of the boat.

Arriving at Wee Cumbrae jetty beside the castle and mansion house. The tide is low uncovering the strand over to Castle Island. This area was known as *the farm side* of the island.

The landing jetty beside the castle, Little Cumbrae House and two garden cottages. Depending on the tide it is easily accessible by small boat. Underfoot is rather rough and not suitable for those with walking difficulties. The three orange coloured floats to the left of the jetty mark the position of creels to catch lobster or prawn. Directly ahead the town of Millport can be seen, approximately one mile distance.

Beside the jetty is this excellent picnic and barbecue area. The authors John and Noreen Steele with photographer Graham Wilson enjoyed lunch here whilst planning how best to use their six hours ashore.

The castle entrance is on the first level via the staircase. At one time there was a drawbridge over a deep ditch. The castle layout comprised of hall, kitchen, chamber, lower western chamber, high western chamber, low eastern chamber, wardrobe, brew-house and vaults.

The huge fireplace is in the main chamber, which also served as a day room and bedroom. Adjoining this room was the kitchen. A report dated 1599 stated the kitchen utensils comprised of two brass pots, two pans, two spits, a pair of hand-irons, an iron ladle, a dozen and a half plates. There were also knives, forks and spoons for six people.

The small internal staircase continues up to the higher levels in the castle and on up to the roof. Another staircase leads down into the dungeon.

The authors on the castle roof. The outlook in every direction is uninterrupted. The castle was strategically positioned to ensure no enemy ship could have approached unnoticed.

The view from the castle roof. The panoramic views are magnificent. Here looking north towards Millport Bay across the stretch of water known as The Tan.

The mansion known as Little Cumbrae House is sheltered by the high cliff behind. It was originally a farm house. Through the years various additions and alterations have been carried out resulting in this imposing mansion. Spectacular views are afforded of the castle and over the Firth of Clyde to the Ayrshire coast.

View of the castle taken through the doorway of Little Cumbrae House.

The well stocked vegetable garden is expertly looked after. There is a great crop of potatoes, carrot, turnip, onions, beans, herbs and a superb strawberry patch. It must be a joy to garden here. There is also a large greenhouse which holds an abundance of tomatoes and other tender plants.

Exotic figs are even growing in the mansion house conservatory.

The bell on the wall is rung to attract the attention of the caretakers. Roger, a visiting relative of the caretakers, answered our ringing of the bell. Roger is holding our landing fee of £5 per person in his hand.

The cottage garden is a magnificent tapestry of colours from nature's most beautiful wild flowers. Large areas of the island become a magnificent shade of blue in early summer when the wild bluebells emerge.

Caretakers Al and Bonnie Davidson are the sole inhabitants of the island. They live in the Old Garden Cottage with their little dog and two cats. Since coming to the island in 2001 Bonnie and Al have been responsible for the maintenance of the mansion house, the three cottages and the castle. They keep the whole estate in pristine condition and have a never ending battle keeping the paths clear, of invading bracken, by using hand held strimmers. The couple are very keen gardeners as is evident from the photographs. They are very much self sufficient. As well as their garden produce they also keep chickens, geese and guinea fowl. From their cottage window the seals are a constant source of entertainment for Bonnie, who loves when the baby seals are born and start to scramble over the rocks. They find it a thrilling sight to see whales and dolphins swimming close by and they are very content living in their island paradise.

Graham Wilson and John Steele at the crossroad behind the mansion house. Left leads up to the lighthouse, cave and burial ground. Right goes to the beach, pier and Sheenawally Point.

Halfway point up the steep hill. The track has been strimmed or it would be impassable due to the height of the bracken. The hills above the village of Fairlie are clearly seen across the Firth of Clyde.

Further up the footpath is the next crossroad. To the left is the burial ground and cave but the bracken has encroached over the track making it virtually impossible to go in that direction. To the right is on up to the lighthouse. The poles which carried the overhead electric supply across the island still stand.

The nests that are scattered on the ground are safe since the rats were completely eradicated. A programme commenced in April 2004 to rid the island of its rat population. The pest control company completed the task in May 2005.

One of the many small chicks scampering about fearlessly. This one even scrambled over Noreen's boot.

This small picturesque loch is a perfect haven for the wild life which live undisturbed on the island. Due to the island's serenity it is a haven for more than 60 species of birds. The Arctic Tern is a regular summer visitor. The Terns come all the way from the Antarctic and start to arrive for their summer stay during May. In the autumn they begin the long journey back to their winter quarters. Another summer visitor is the House Martin from Africa, where they spend the winter. These little birds feed on aerial insects during their long flight from Africa to this special little island. The Whooper Swan, from Iceland, is a winter visitor. The swans arrive in the autumn and find a suitable small sheltered loch to roost on. The shallow water rarely freezes over and the surrounding pastures provide for these winter visitors.

The old original lighthouse stands well preserved on the hilltop. The flame from the coal fire could be seen from the shipping channels on both sides of the island.

The plaque fixed above the doorway of the tower. The last line reads in Latin Ostendimus Litora Flammis translated is; *Flames Light The Coast*.

Inside the tower the remains of the circular staircase are very evident. It is incredible that the tons of coal necessary to keep the fire burning had to be carried manually up the staircase to the iron basket at the top.

The colourful Lichen growing on the rocks testifies to the purity of the air.

The principle keeper was always housed in the cottage adjacent to the lighthouse. A door in the cottage gave direct access into the lighthouse. On the cottage roof the ornamental chimney-top has stood the test of time.

View inside the now disused lighthouse. A metal ladder fixed to the wall gives access to the platform surrounding the windows. Interestingly the wall beside the ladder is decorated with ornamental plasterwork.

The dismantled foghorn is still on the island. It was no longer required thanks to sophisticated satellite navigation and state-of-the-art radar. When in operation the fog signal was three blasts, silence for 35 seconds. Two blasts. Silence for 35 seconds then the sequence was repeated.

Inside the Horn House the main generator and the emergency generator stand idle. They were in use for many years compressing air and pumping it into the storage tanks which are situated outside the building. The emergency generator was on standby in case the main generator failed or was due its annual maintenance.

When the fog horn was required the duty lighthouse keeper would switch on the main generator. The compressed air in the storage tanks was forced into the fog horn which gave out the loud drone that could be heard up to eight miles distant.

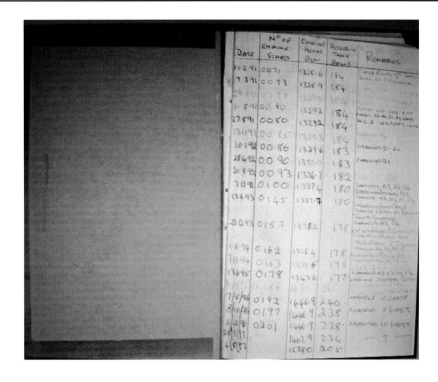

The Horn House register is where all maintenance was recorded. The page shows the date of each visit, the number of times the generator engine was started, the number of hours it was run, the amount of diesel contained in the storage tank and a column for remarks. The remarks column states on different dates; *Engine in good order. Changed ten lamps. Engine battery tested. Changed diesel.*
The last entry of 6th August 1997 records: *205 gallons of diesel in the storage tank.*

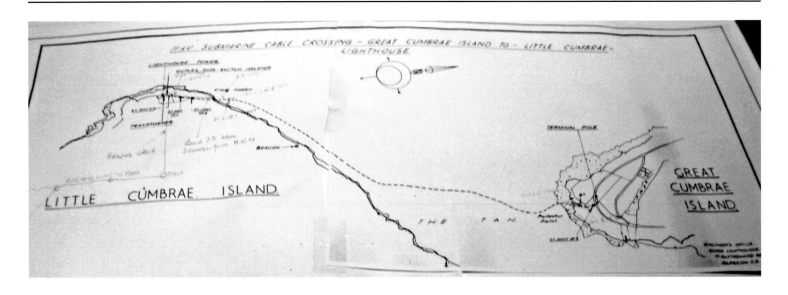

In 1952 Clyde Lighthouses signed a contract for the laying of a heavy duty electric cable from Great Cumbrae to Wee Cumbrae. The cable was 3341 yards long, almost two miles.

The project commenced on the 8th April 1957. From Great Cumbrae the cable was laid on the seabed across to the shore on Wee Cumbrae then hugging the shoreline, still under water, until reaching Craig Nabbin, on the north west coast.

From there the cable came ashore to power the lighthouse, the keepers houses and the foghorn building. The electric supply then extended overhead to the opposite coast and down to the mansion and cottages. Work was completed in four weeks on the 8th May 1957.

Eight years later, in January 1965, the cable was damaged and took three days to repair. It was suspected the damage had been caused by a fishing boat. This happened on a number of occasions until in 1997 the cable broke.

As the cost of replacing the heavy duty cable was in excess of £250,000 Clyde Lighthouses decided to replace the lighthouse with a small single light prominently situated on the roof of the nearby foghorn building. Nineteen solar panels were shipped to the island to power the new light.

The nineteen solar panels charge five banks of batteries stored in the fog horn building. The batteries power the single navigation light positioned on the roof of the horn building.

The tanks behind the solar panels previously stored the compressed air that operated the fog horn.

The new navigation light is positioned high up in the background.

The present day 12 volt navigation light which replaced the lighthouse. The light is classed as a Shore Light and is fixed to a metal pole. The light sequence is a one second flash every six seconds.
It has a 12 Volt, 107 Watt flashing lamp. A Photo Cell ensures it activates between dusk and dawn. The light is numbered 4346 on Admiralty charts.
In the background is the southern part of the island of Bute. The north of Arran can be seen in the far distance.

The old mill wheel makes an attractive picnic table. It stands beside the lighthouse complex and is positioned at a magnificent view point. The two large rocks standing behind the table resemble faces looking in different directions.

Looking back at the castle from high on the hillside. In the far distance across the water from Cumbrae Castle can be seen Portencross Castle. The two castles are almost identical.

Sheenawally Point is the most northerly point of Wee Cumbrae. Looking across *The Tan* to Millport. This is the shortest distance between the two islands.

The end of a perfect day exploring Wee Cumbrae. Noreen Steele and Graham Wilson waiting for the boat back to Largs.

The whole population of Wee Cumbrae have come to bid us fairwell from their tranquil little island.

After arriving safely back at Largs, we watched *Silver Spray*, a well maintained charter boat, sail back to her moorings in Largs Bay.

Lighthouse on clifftop

In the past the lighthouse complex has been home to many families. The light keepers were kept busy attending to their duties. They were dedicated to keeping the lighthouse functioning.

It is difficult to comprehend how one single automatic light can replace all the people who were involved and lived within the lighthouse complex. Now the lighthouse, workshop and family homes all stand empty; left only with the memories of a bygone era. Beside the now deserted jetties stands a forlorn notice which states:

WILDLIFE RESERVE
NO ACCESS

Reviews

This book is a unique insight, through personal reminiscences and original photographs of what it was like for the lighthouse keepers with their families to live on the beautiful, little-known island of Wee Cumbrae.
Jill McColl
The Vennel Local and Family History Centre
North Ayrshire Council

Another exhaustive and thoroughly researched work from Ardrossan based authors John and Noreen Steele, who have produced many fascinating books.
Their greatest achievement, involving years of painstaking and meticulous detective work, was to uncover the dark secrets of the shocking tragedy of British aircraft carrier, HMS Dasher, sunk off Ardrossan just south of Wee Cumbrae in 1943 with the loss of 379 lives.
Wee Cumbrae is now the subject of their latest book. This takes the reader on a voyage of discovery revealing intriguing hidden secrets from the 7th century. The people of this seldom visited island are also brought to life revealing the interesting stories of lighthouse keepers and their families and gripping tales of the many shipwrecks on and around the island.
Donald L Reid. Author and local historian. Beith.

ISBN 978-0-9532637-0-7

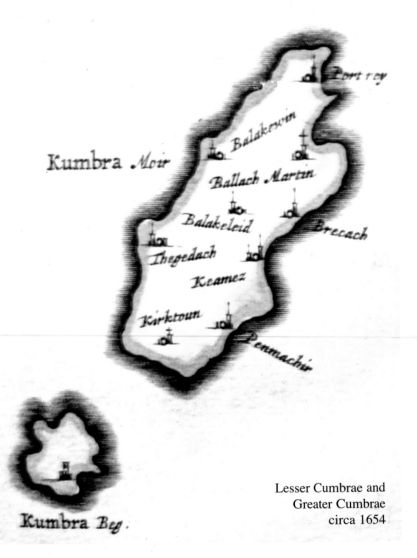

Lesser Cumbrae and
Greater Cumbrae
circa 1654